M3 Mathematics
MAPPING MATHEMATICAL MEANING

Polygons

Helen Pengelly

ASHTON SCHOLASTIC
SYDNEY AUCKLAND NEW YORK TORONTO LONDON

The purchase of this book entitles the teacher to reproduce
the blackline masters for classroom use.

Text copyright © Helen Pengelly, 1991.
Copyright © Ashton Scholastic Pty Limited, 1991.

First published in 1991 by Ashton Scholastic Pty Limited A.C.N. 000 614 577,
PO Box 579, Gosford 2250. Also in Brisbane, Melbourne, Adelaide, Perth and
Auckland, NZ.

All rights reserved. No part of this publication may be reproduced or
transmitted in any form or by any means, electronic or mechanical, including
photocopying, recording, storage in an information retrieval system, or
otherwise, without the prior written permission of the publisher, unless
specifically permitted under the Australian Copyright Act 1968 as amended.

Typeset by David Lake Typesetting, Forresters Beach NSW.
Printed by Globalcom Pty Ltd, Singapore.
Typeset in Helvetica.

12 11 10 9 8 7 6 5 4 3 2 1   1 2 3 4 5 / 9

Setting the context

This book is one in a series of books addressing mathematics curricula in the primary school years. Collectively, the books outline an approach to the teaching and learning of mathematics. Their purpose is to inform, support and resource teachers when planning, implementing and reviewing their mathematics programs.

Giving information about the rationale, content and methodology in a conceptual rather than a procedural way enables teachers to build a curriculum which is responsive to the needs of individual children, the class, the school and the school community. The materials do not provide a program in the traditional sense of setting learning out in a linear and prescribed manner through student books and teacher guides. They do provide teachers with a framework to build a mathematics curriculum which reflects the rationale and methodology of the different education department policy guidelines. Learning mathematics becomes a personal, interactive process negotiated between the policy statements of the institution and the school, the interests, abilities and reactions of the children in a class, and the teacher's belief, knowledge and practices.

One book discusses the principles underlying this approach to mathematics teaching. Six topic books give an account of these theories in action. They describe the nature and type of activities which give children personal experiences with mathematics. The books outline an ongoing process of planning for and responding to children's mathematical learning.

In another collection of books in this series, a group of teachers write about how they implemented this approach. Their books on getting started, on planning and programming, on assessment, evaluation and reporting, and on the role of language and interaction in mathematics learning, are practical accounts of organisation and management strategies. Books in the fourth category are to be used to resource students' mathematical learning in an active way.

How to use
Polygons

Mathematics can be defined as the science of number and space. Measuring space and knowing about shapes are both central to the primary mathematics curriculum. Children have to experience concepts relating to space and shape through their own explorations with mathematical models. These models provide tangible manipulative pieces for children to build, compare and contrast. As a result of these investigations, they develop ideas and test hypotheses.

When programs focus on children's personal experiences with mathematical models, a teacher can attend to each child's thinking and relate that to the mathematical ideas outlined in syllabus statements. Building teaching procedures around children's thinking places the emphasis on the personal experiences each child has with mathematics. In this approach, learning about shapes and the relationships between them depends on what teachers set up for children to do.

This book has a range of shapes including triangles, quadrilaterals, pentagons, hexagons and other concave and convex polygons. Some are regular, some irregular. Each page is meant to be photocopied so that the individual shapes can be cut out and used as models for children to work with. It may be best to photocopy them onto cardboard as cardboard is easier for children to manipulate.

Giving children access to their own sets of materials is important. It enables them to form and check their ideas. In the beginning it is advisable to use materials that are easy to manipulate, namely wooden blocks, foam shapes and other sets of commercially available materials. As the mathematical ideas become established, and as motor skills develop, children can work with the more compact shapes this book provides.

The range of shapes that exists in commercial sets is very narrow. Rectangles tend to always have proportions similar to the 'golden ratio'. Long, thin rectangles, for example, are rarely included in sets of shapes, and squares are seen in a category of their own rather than as a subset of the set of rectangles. Access to such limited models of any particular shape can lead children to incorrect conclusions. The greater range of shapes in this set is intended to supplement existing materials and give children the range of resources they need to make valid generalisations about the properties of shapes and the relationships between them.

Sorting shapes

Many of the concepts outlined in the spatial strand of curriculum documents can be developed through sorting and classifying shapes. (This is described in detail in other books in this series, including *Classification, a process of learning mathematics*; *Mathematics, a search for **Patterns*** and ***Measuring Space***.)

When first starting to classify shapes, children tend to sort them according to their number of sides and corners. In doing this, they learn the names of shapes and the characteristics that make them fit certain categories. It is important not to overload a student with too many shapes. Always select the ones that seem appropriate for the activity and the concepts that are to be explored. Unless children experience a comprehensive collection of three-sided figures, for example, they may think that all triangles resemble the proportions of an equilateral one. Giving children a selection of triangles only to sort, helps them understand the characteristics that determine triangularity. Children also have to distinguish triangles from shapes with more than three sides.

When sorting and resorting various groups of shapes, children learn the properties and names of them as well as how they are measured. They also refine their classification skills. As the characteristics of shapes are identified and as children develop mathematical terminology to describe and discuss these properties, they become more precise in the criteria used to define and record them. In order to do this, children learn how to measure shapes using geometric instruments including the ruler, the compass and the protractor.

Younger children may sort a collection of shapes and find that there are different kinds of quadrilaterals—irregular four-sided shapes, trapezoids (one set of parallel sides) and parallelograms (two sets of parallel sides where the opposite sides are equal). The parallelograms which have adjacent sides also equal are called rhombi (singular, rhombus). Shapes with opposite sides equal and parallel and with angles of 90° are rectangles. Squares form a subset of the set of rectangles because they also have adjacent sides that are equal. Children learn about these categories through classification of shapes which exhibit these differing characteristics. Shapes have to be selected to suit the purpose of an investigation.

If older children are to learn about similarity and congruence, a selection of shapes from the following pages can be photocopied and enlarged or reduced to varying degrees to create shapes which are smaller, larger and the same size as the originals. This forms a set of shapes which exemplify congruence and similarity. The mathematical model is established.

Once cut out, the resulting collection is given to a child to classify. Children make groups of shapes that look the same. From a group of similar shapes children find ones which are exactly the same. The notion of similarity and congruence can be addressed. Different shapes can be photocopied, reduced and enlarged to make other sets. These collections can also be sorted to give children more experience with these concepts.

Children learn to measure angles and sides as a means of becoming more explicit in describing the likenesses and differences between shapes. The continual refinement of this process takes place by resorting the original collection or by sorting and resorting the subgroups. Gradually, a child's attention is drawn to the characteristics of the shapes and the relationships between them. From this, children make generalisations in the form of definitions.

Through sorting and classifying the shapes in this book children can learn to:
- recognise, name and define two-dimensional shapes
- measure angles, length, perimeter and area. From this, children find patterns to predict the sum of interior angles of polygons and the formulae for determining the areas of rectangles and triangles
- use geometric instruments—ruler, compass, and protractor.

Children also learn about diagonals, symmetry, congruence, similarity and tessellations.

One of the ways children record the results of their classifications is to tabulate and graph the data. Skills in graphing develop as a result.

Some of these shapes can also be used to construct three-dimensional models. From this beginning, nets for solids and concepts of surface area, capacity and volume can be developed.

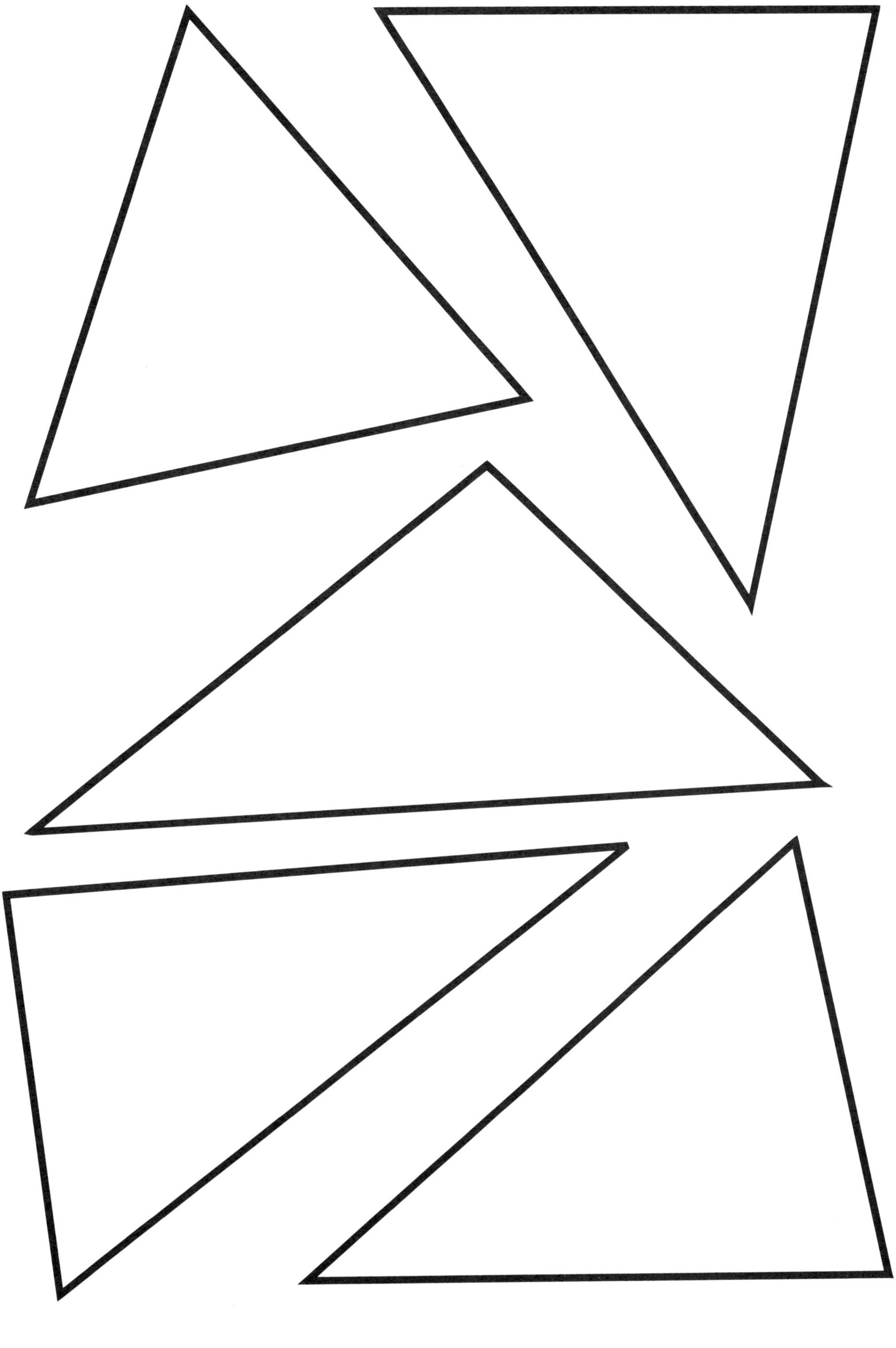

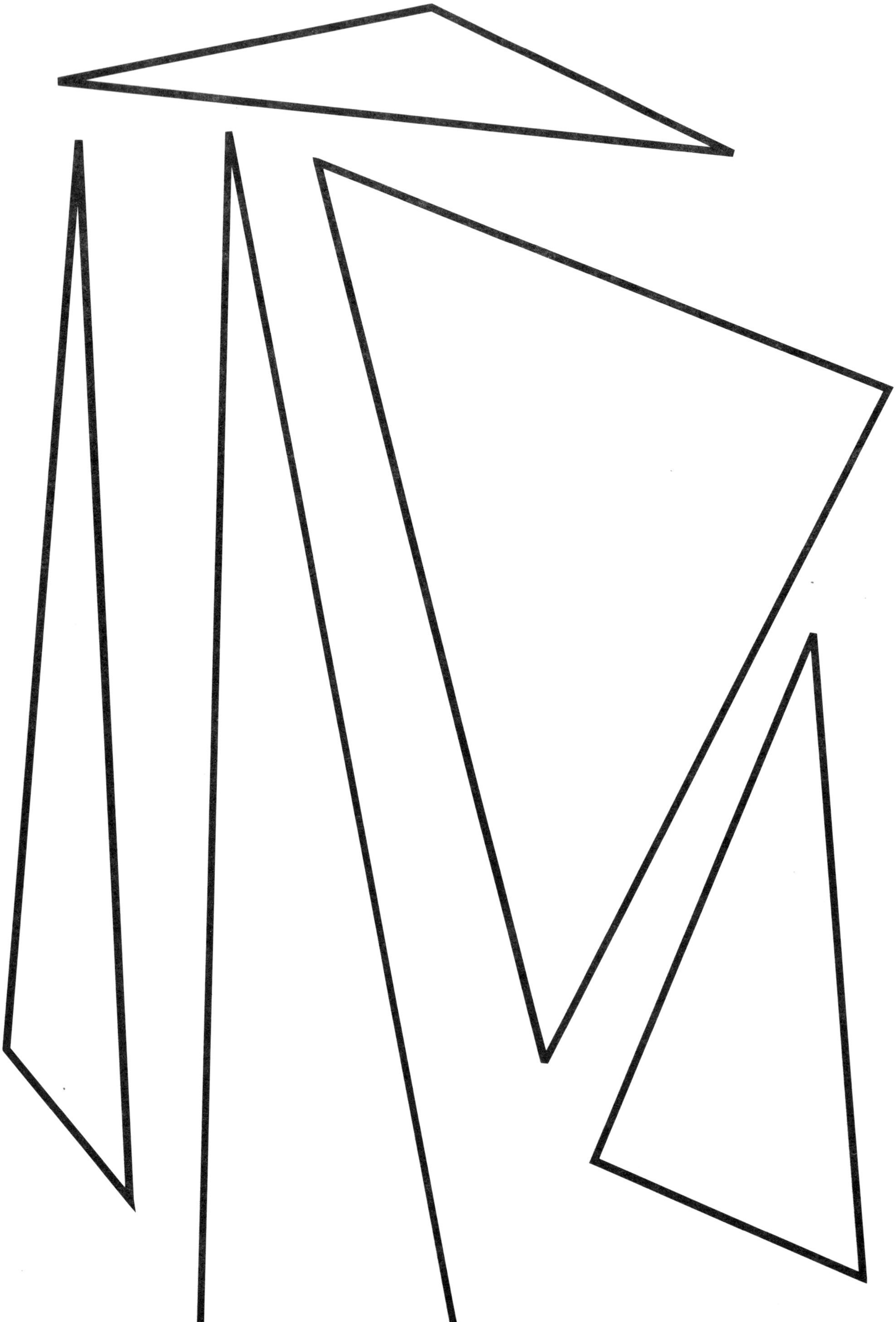

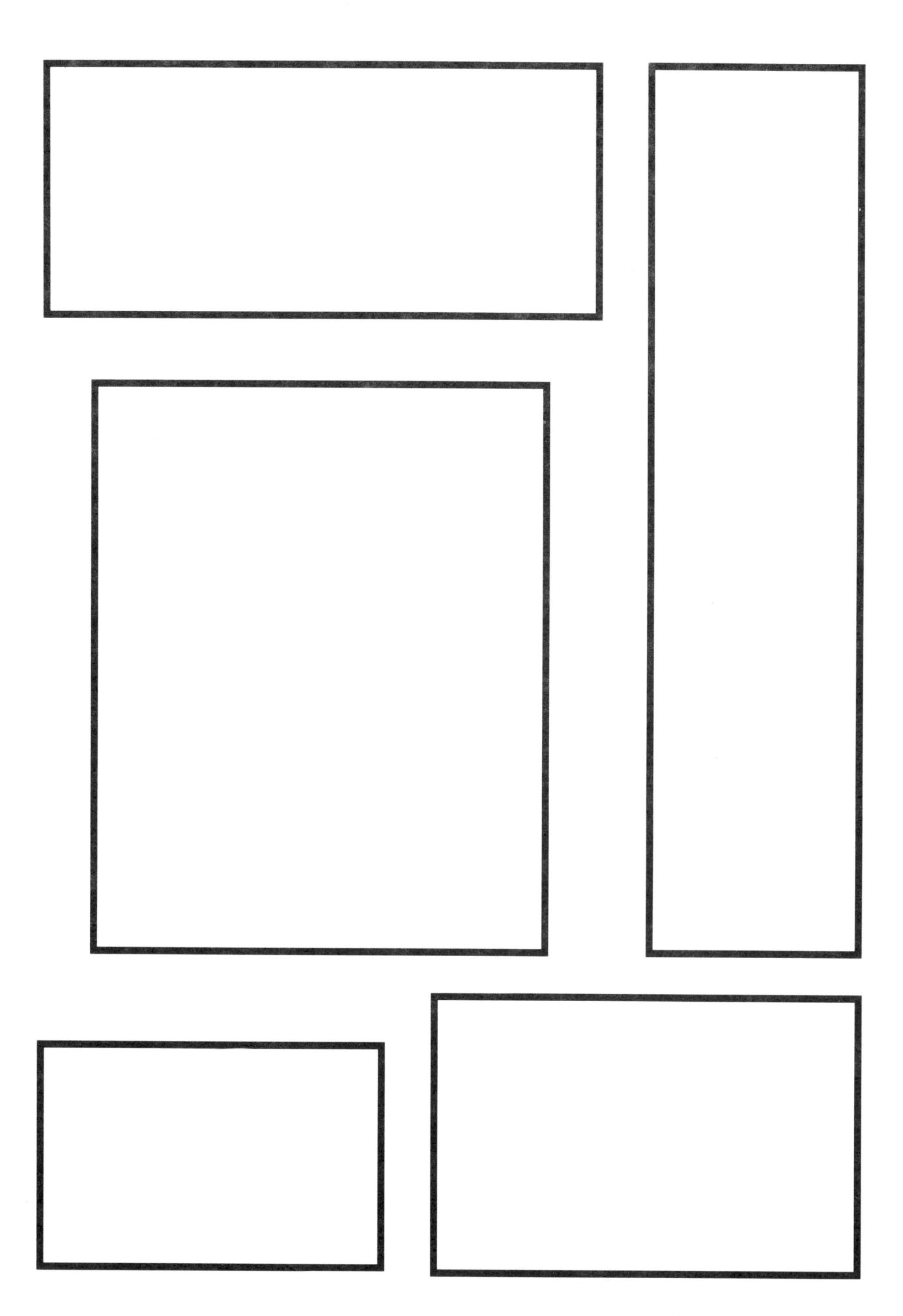

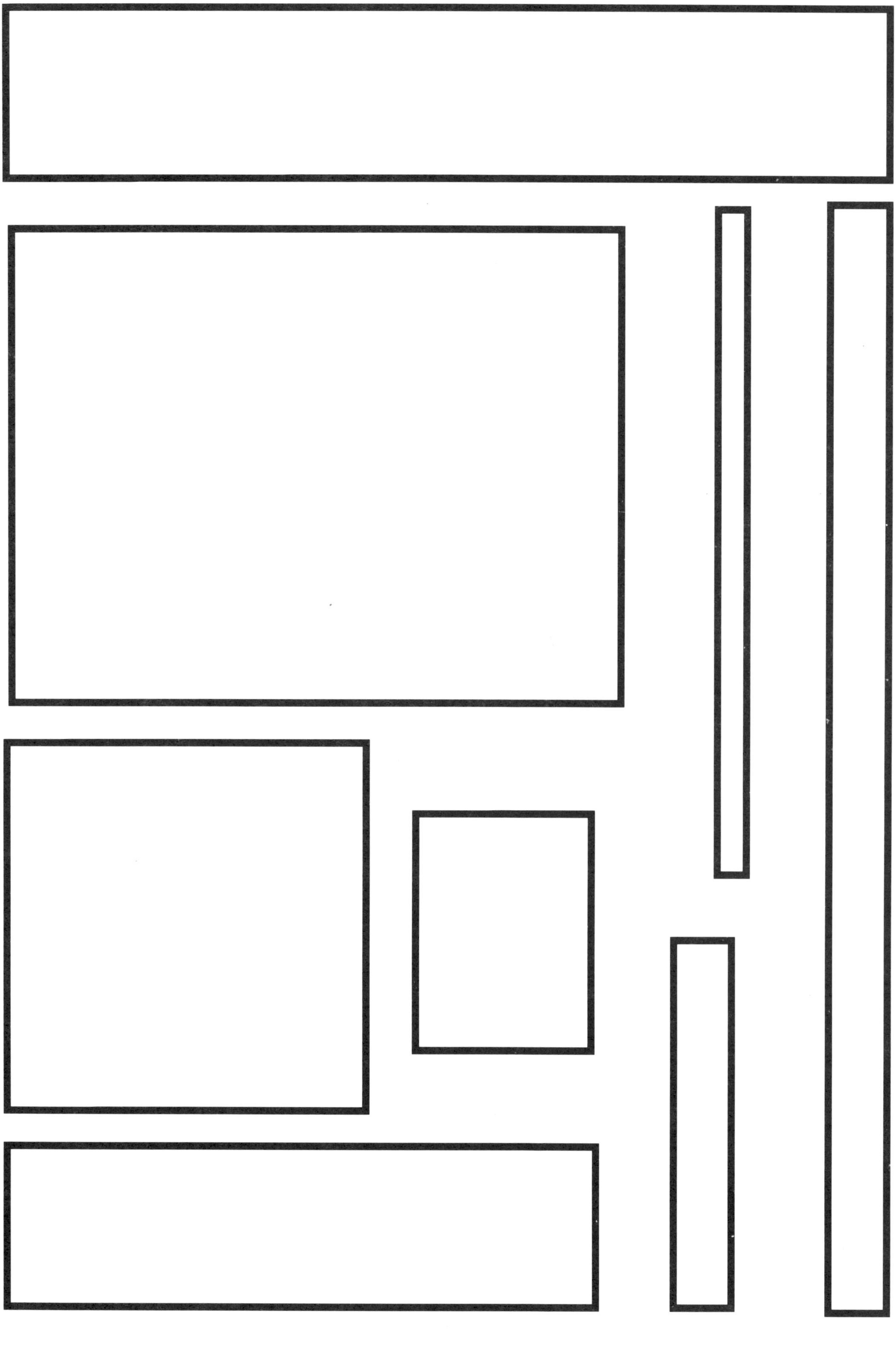

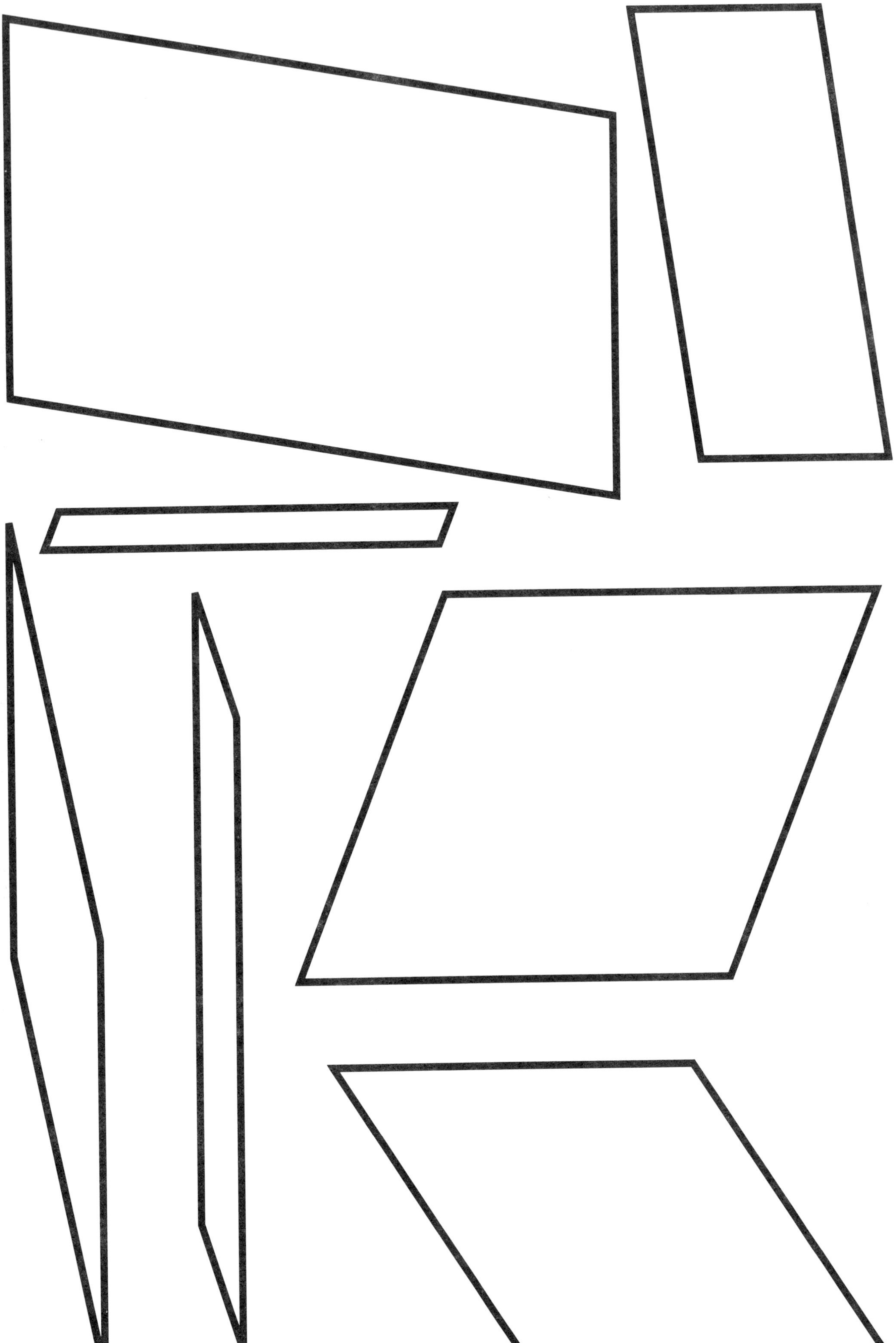

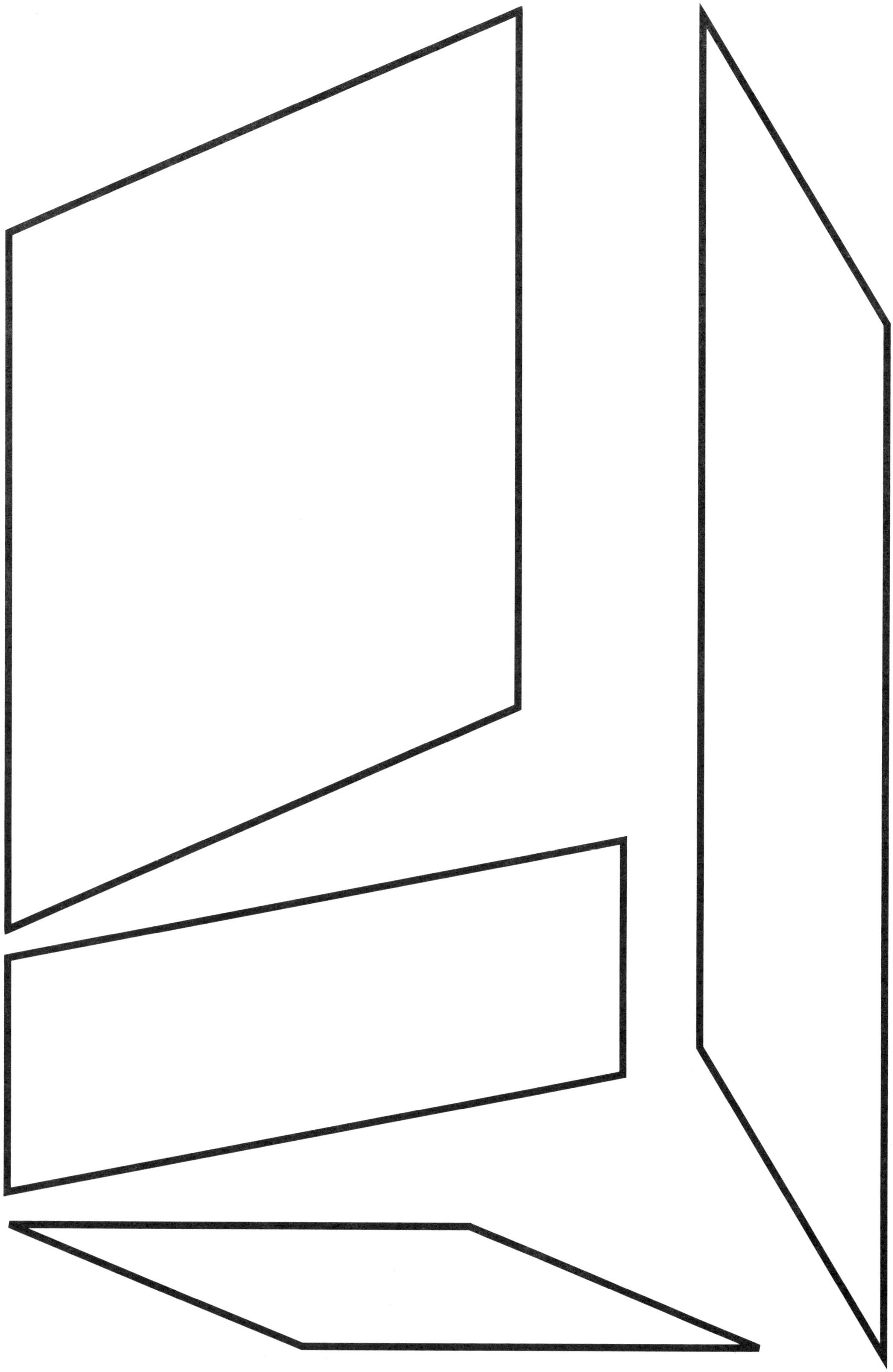

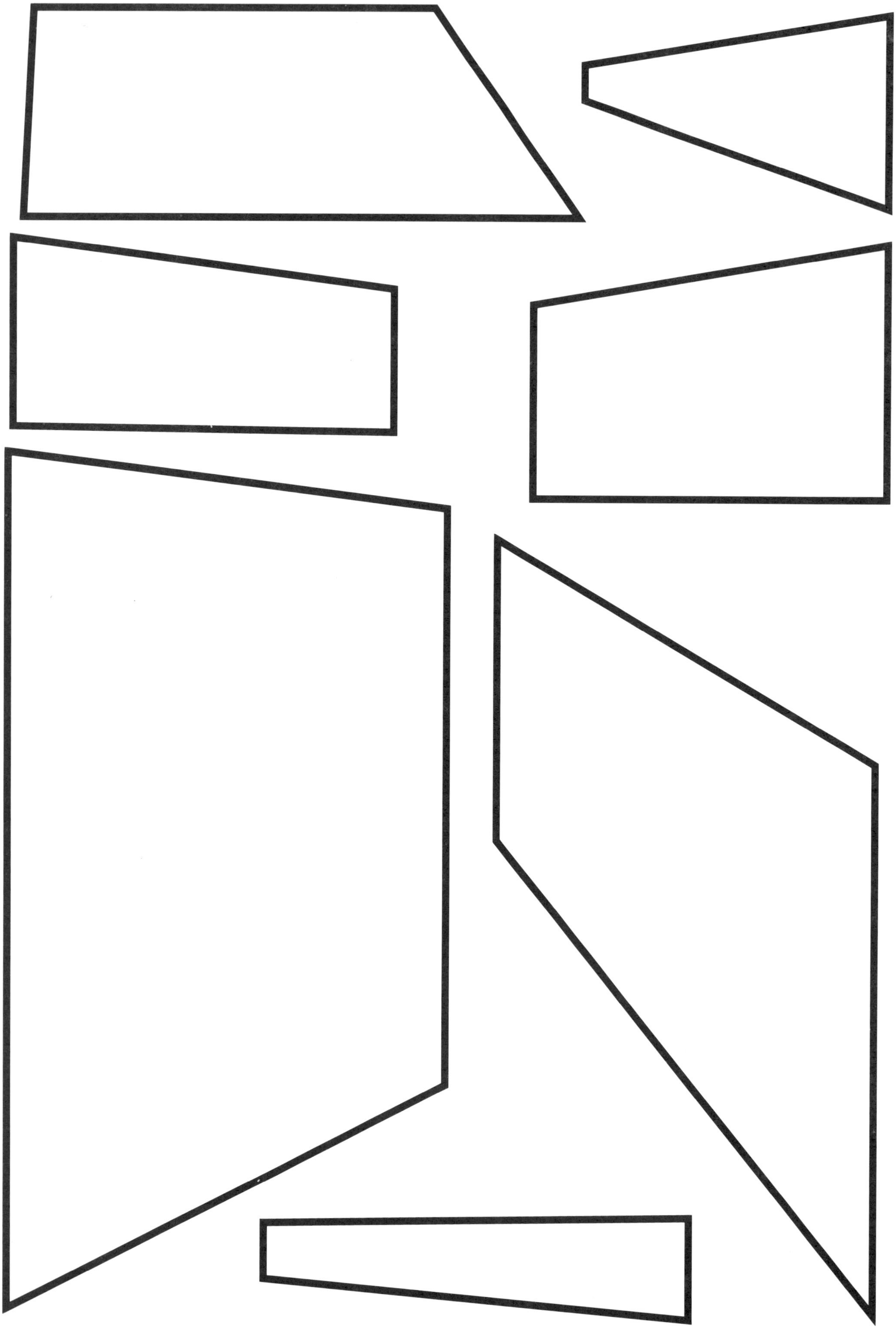

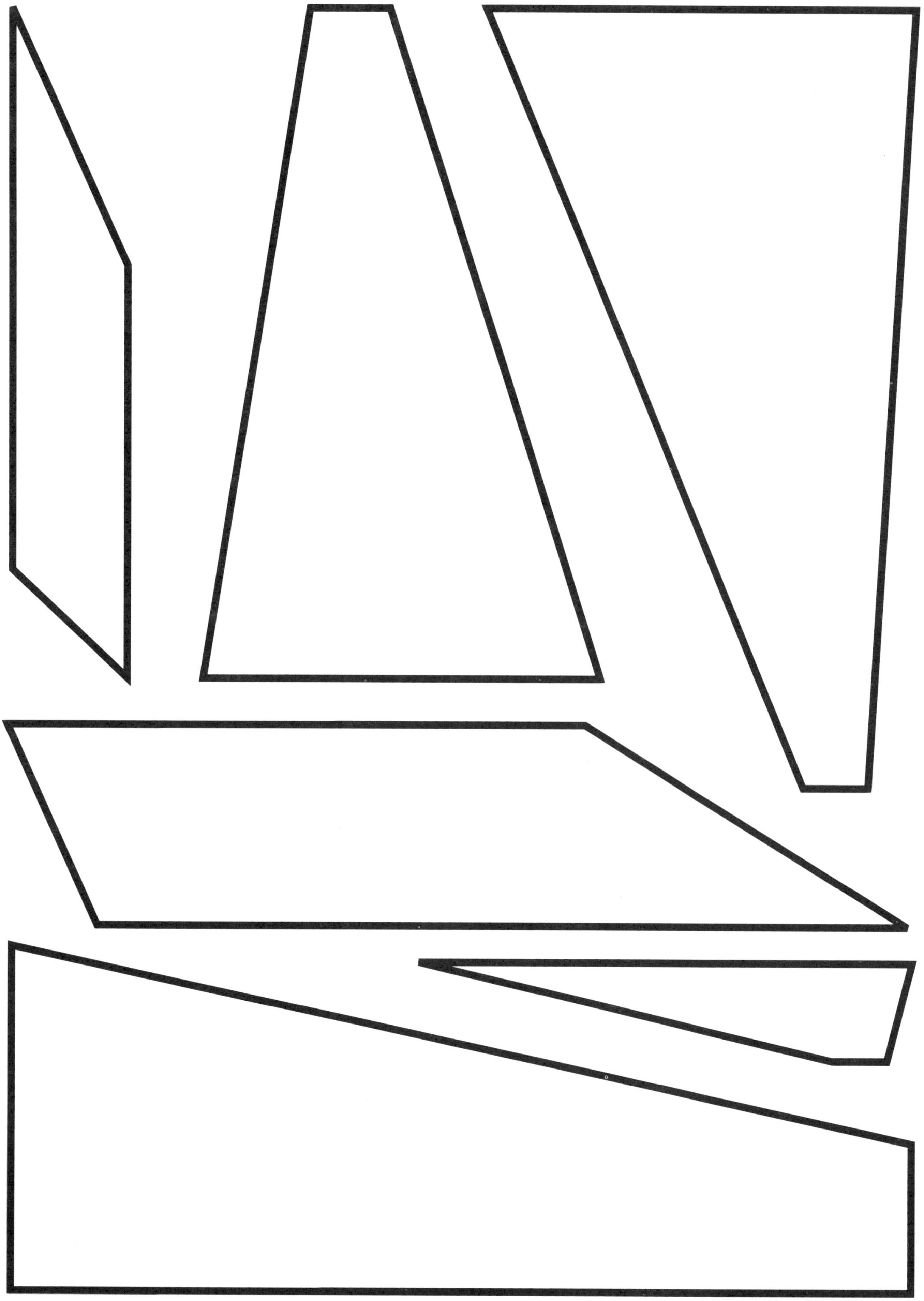

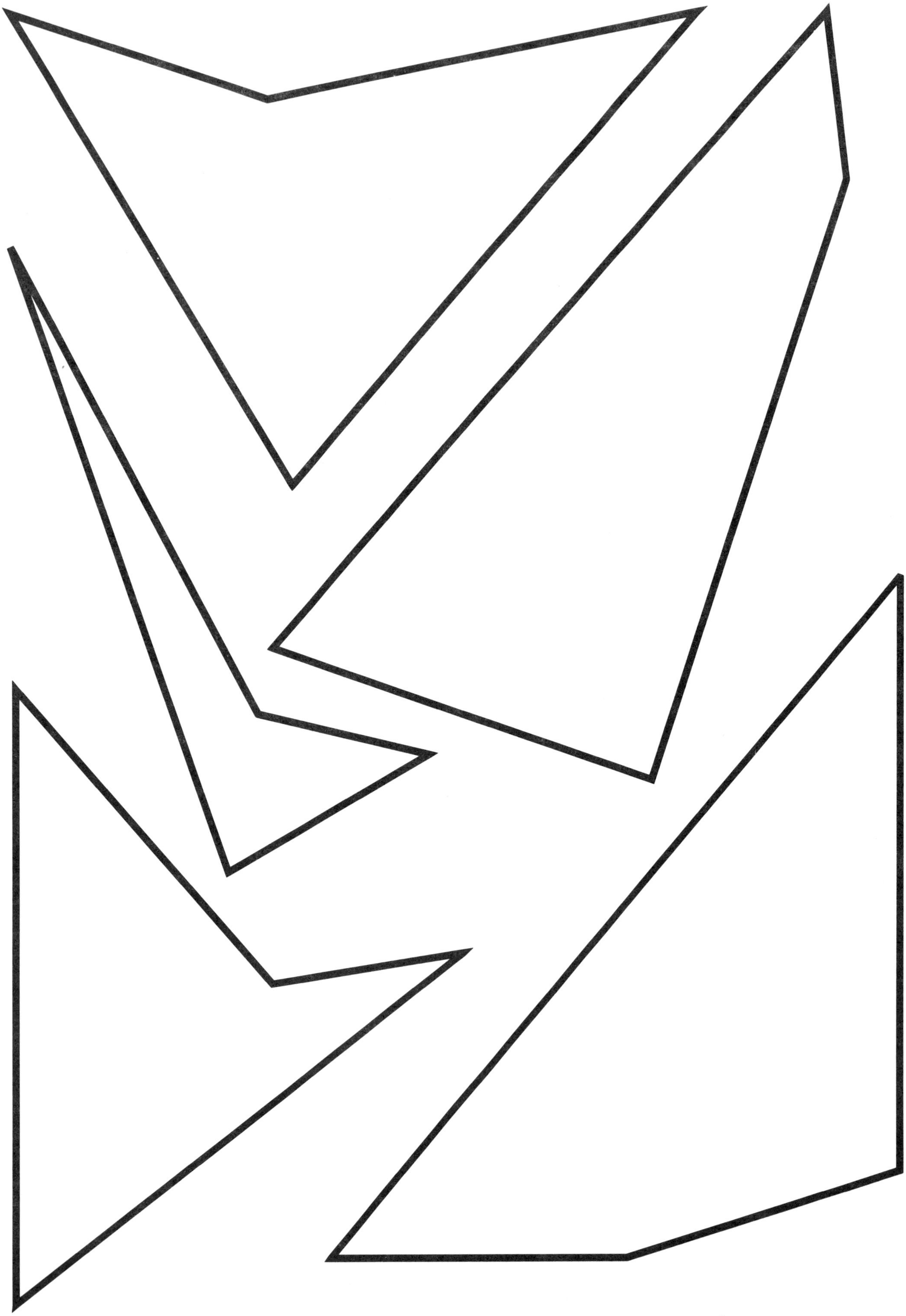

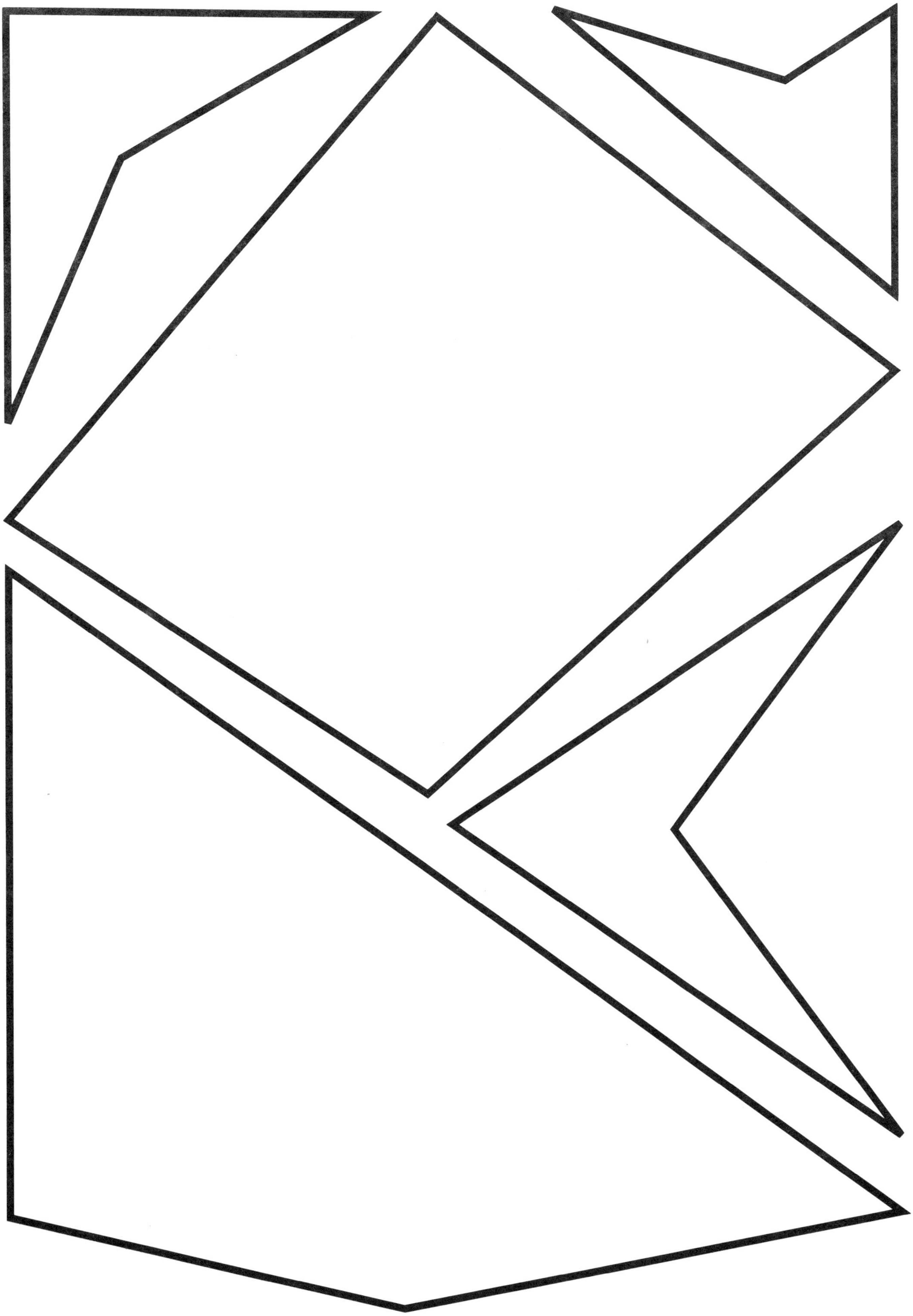

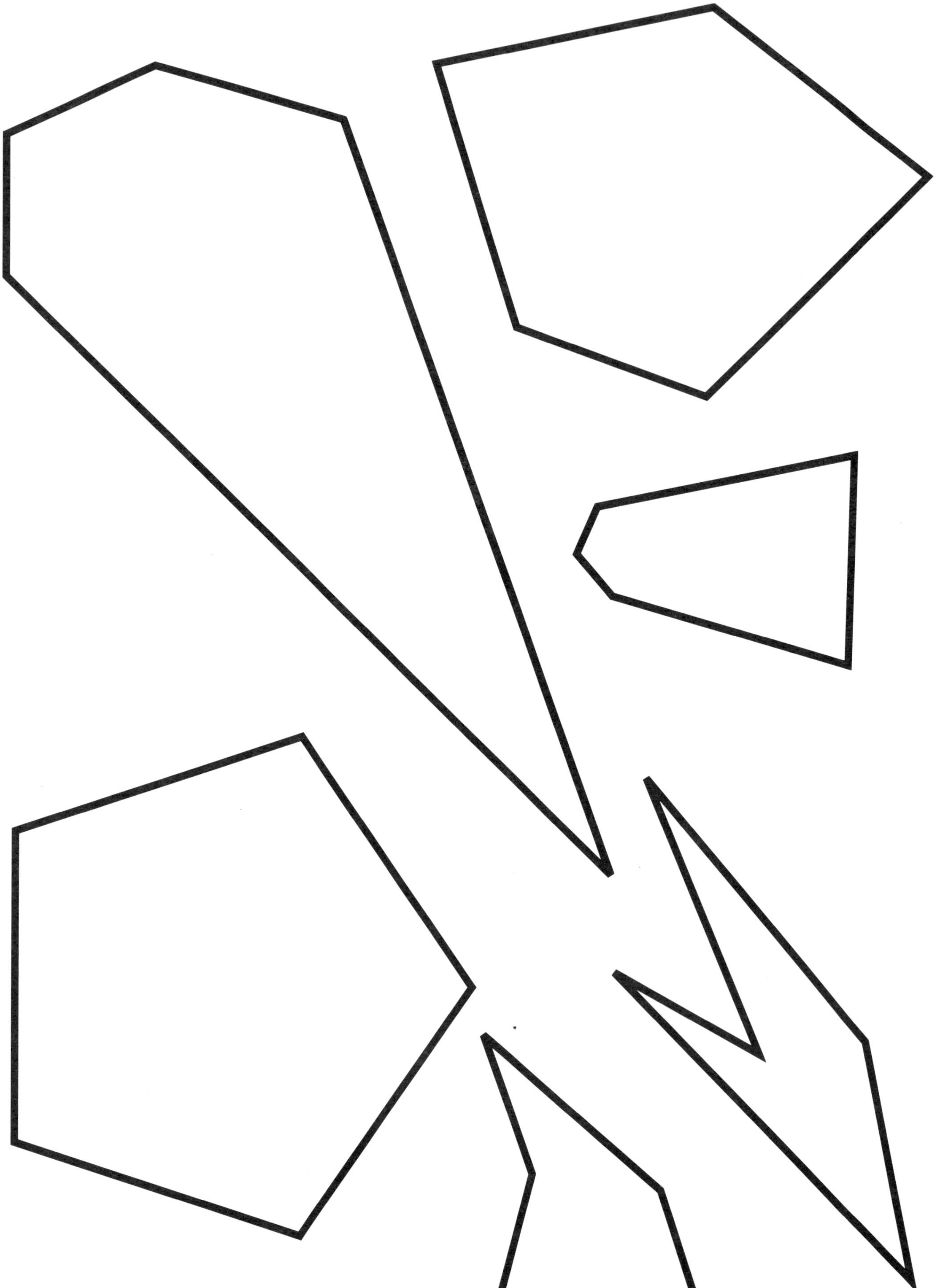

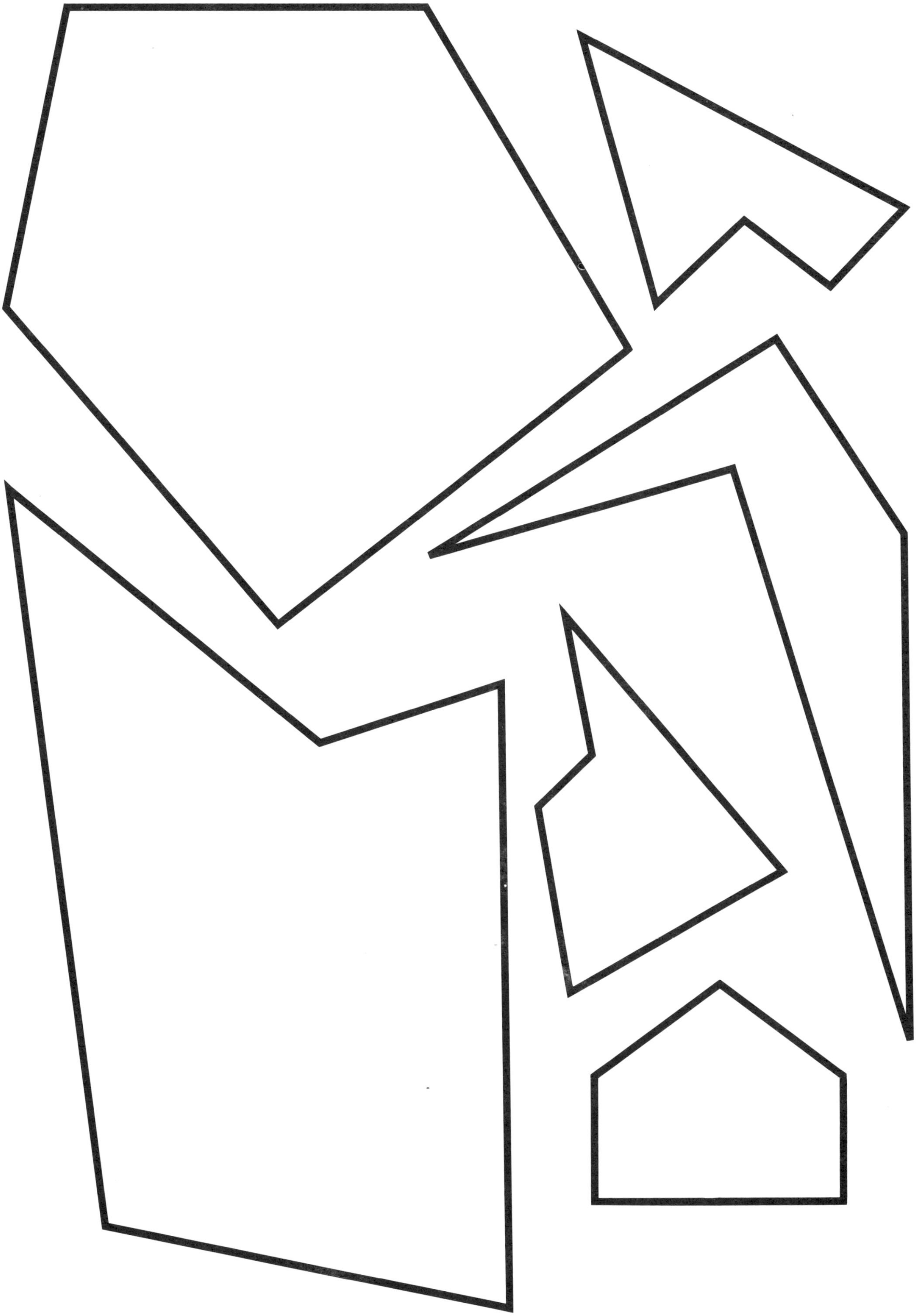

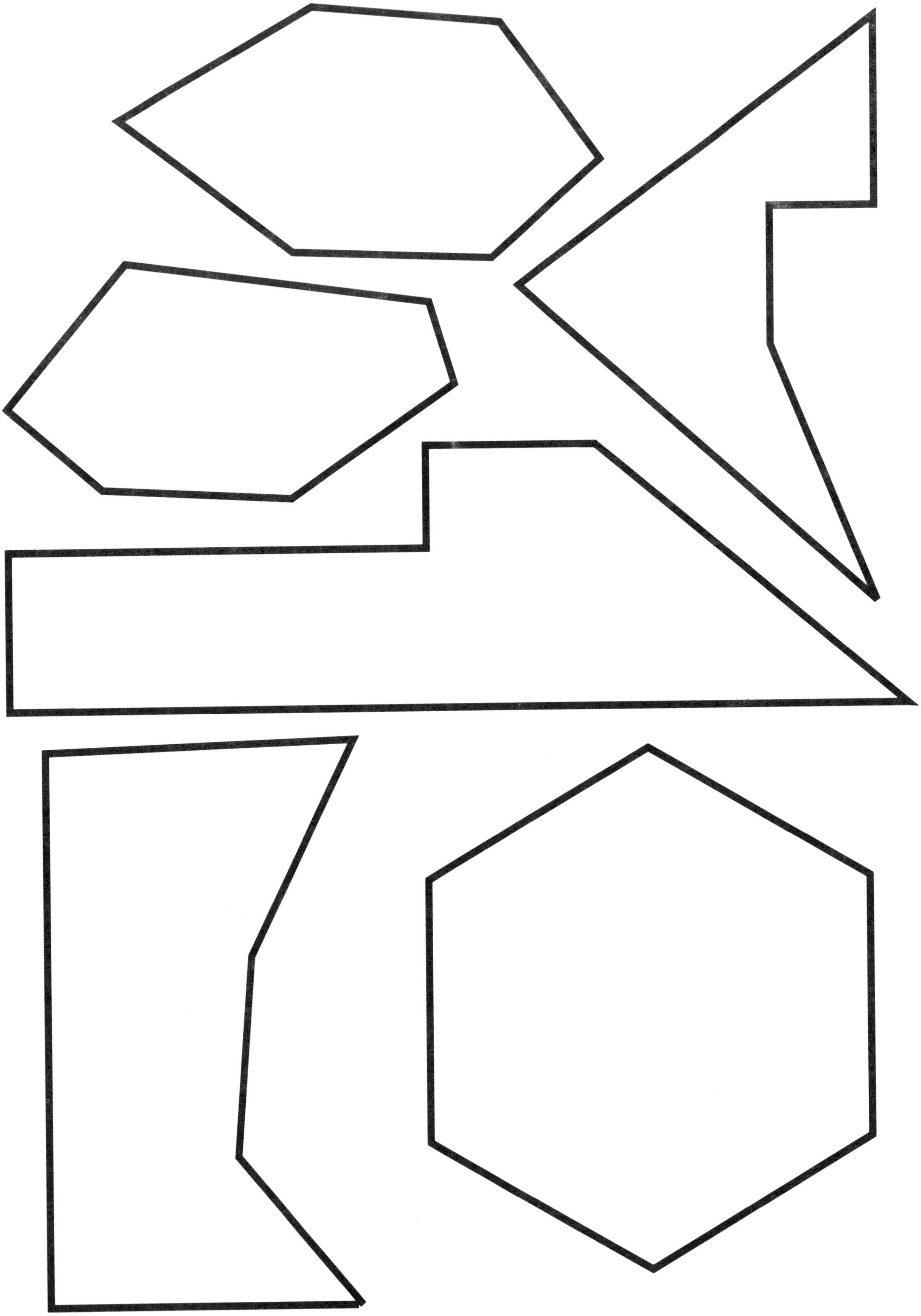

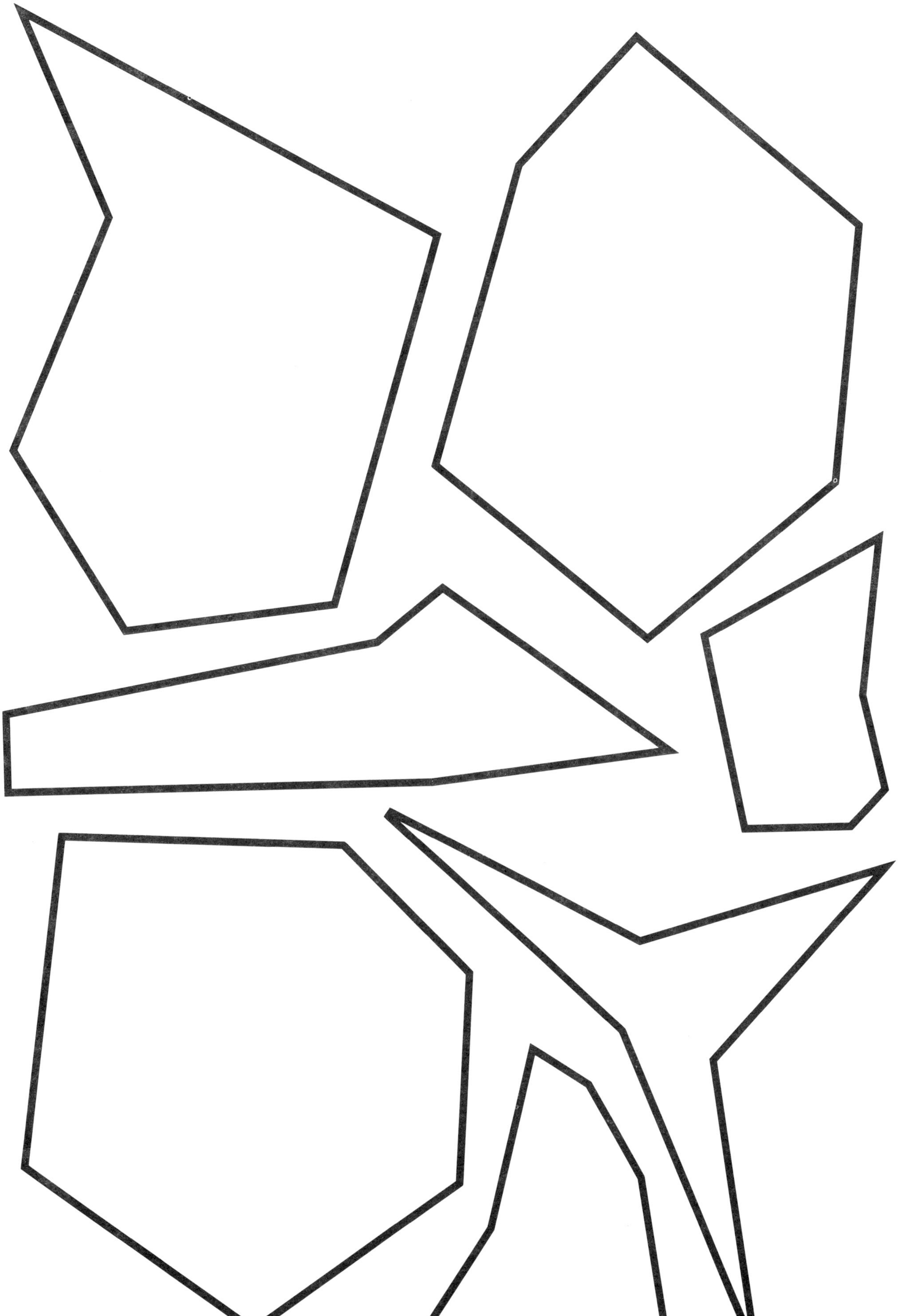

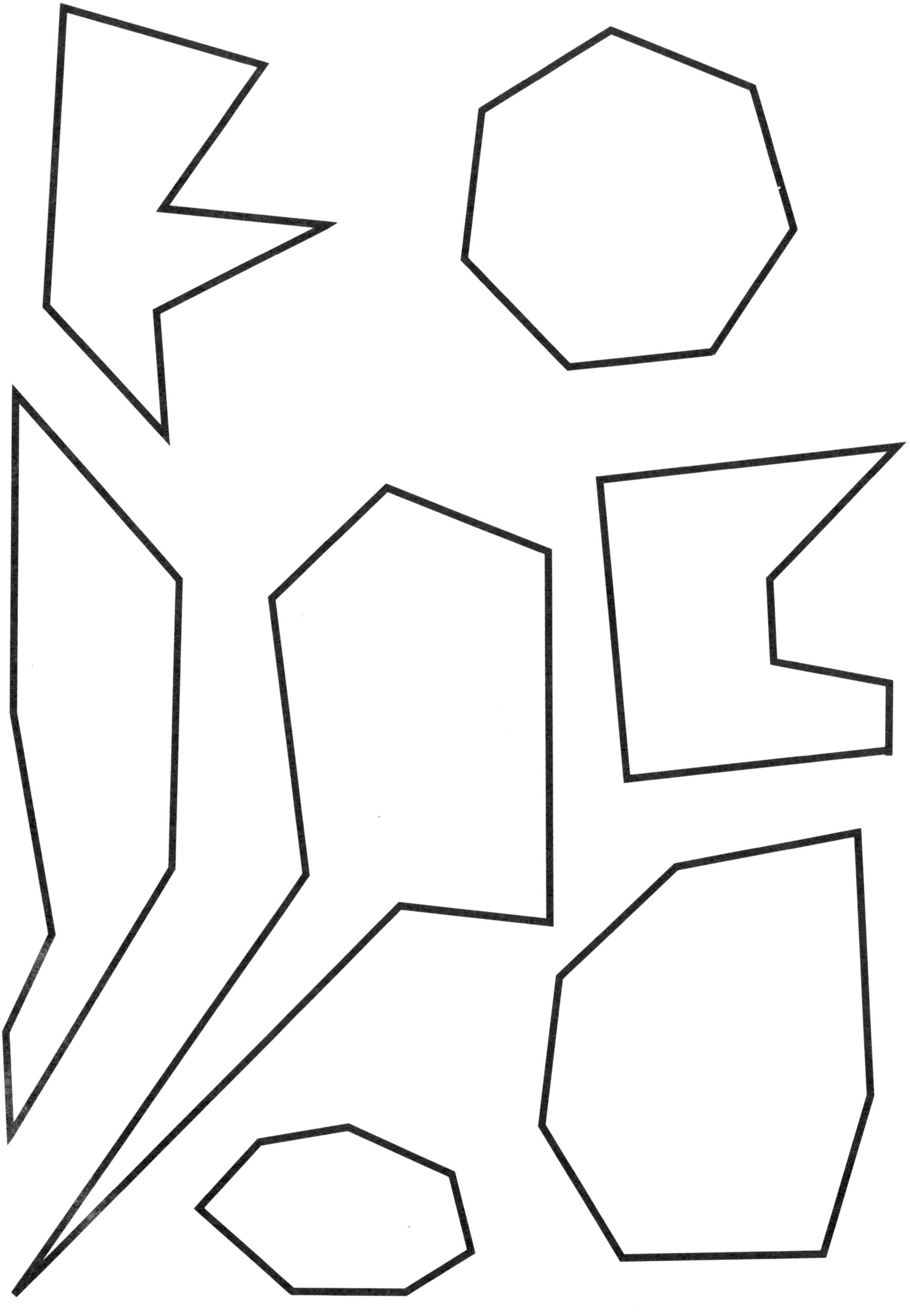

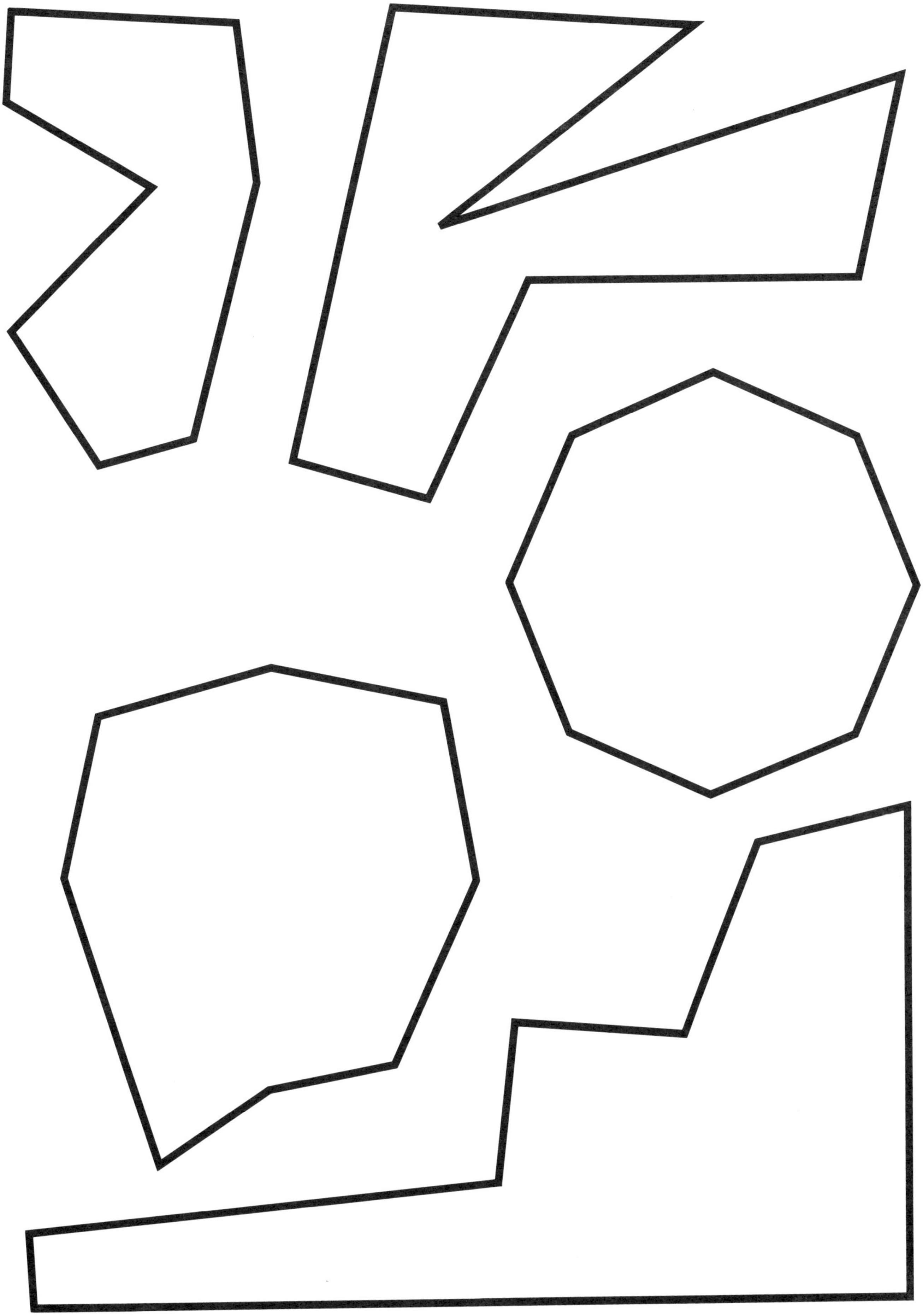

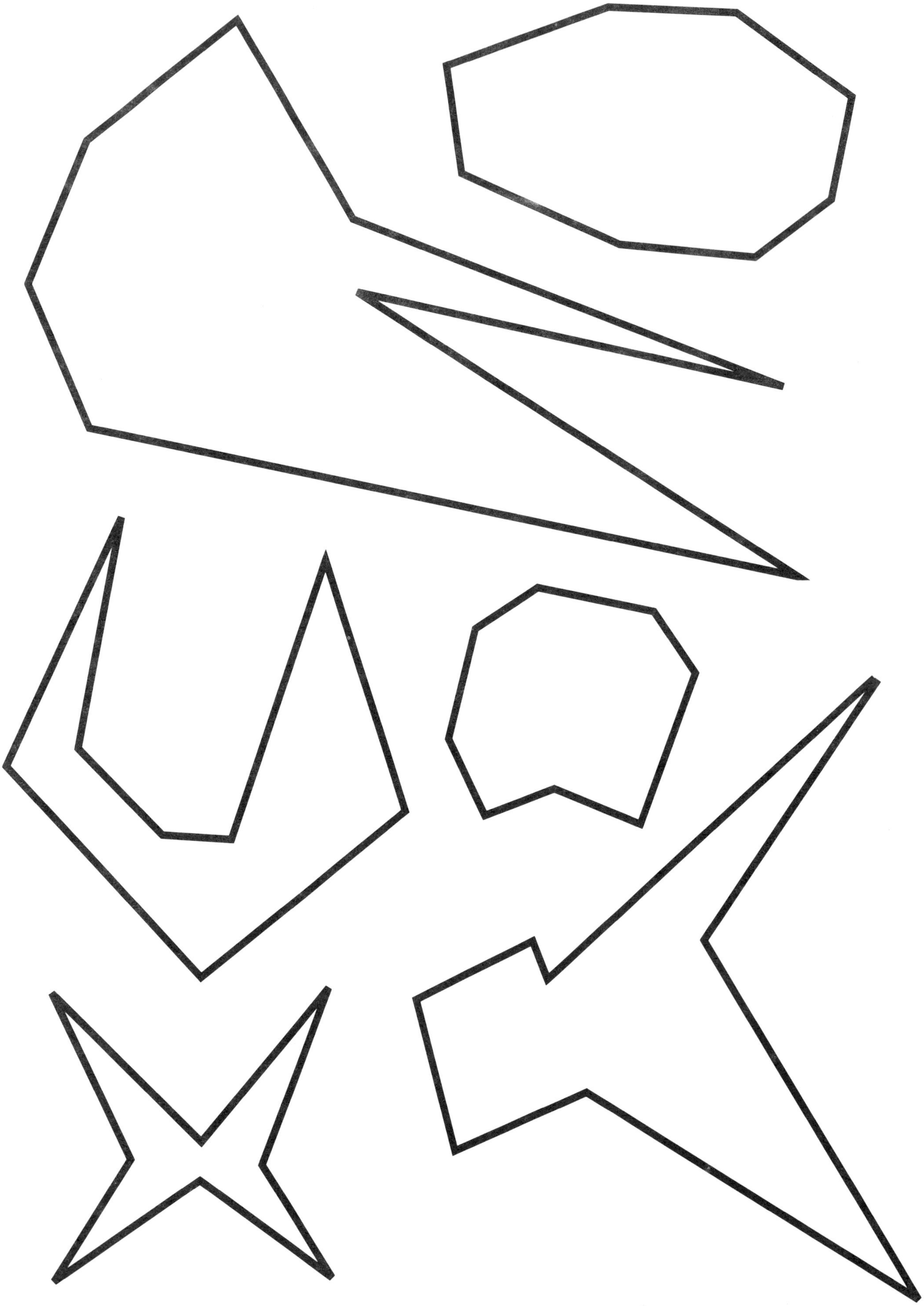

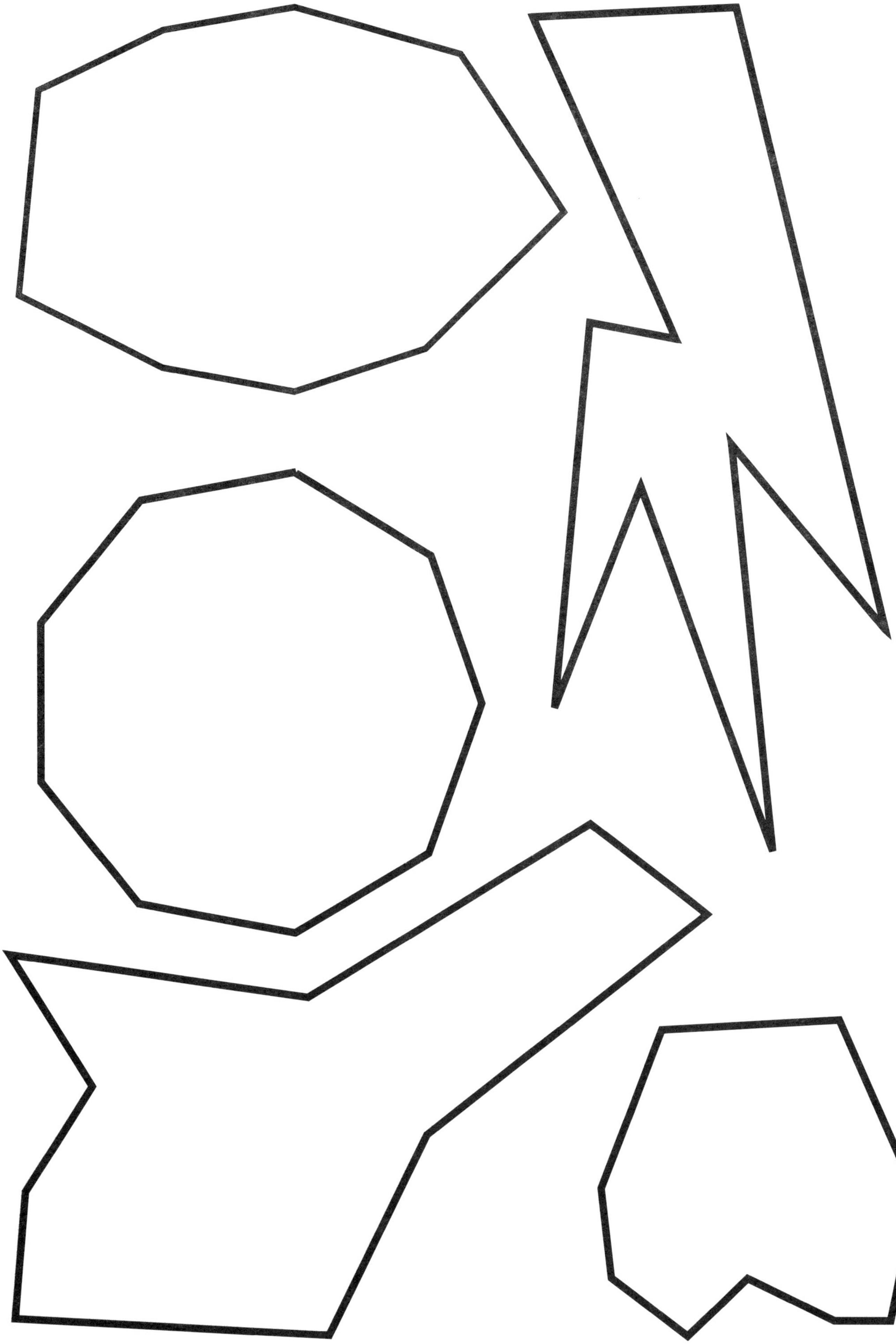

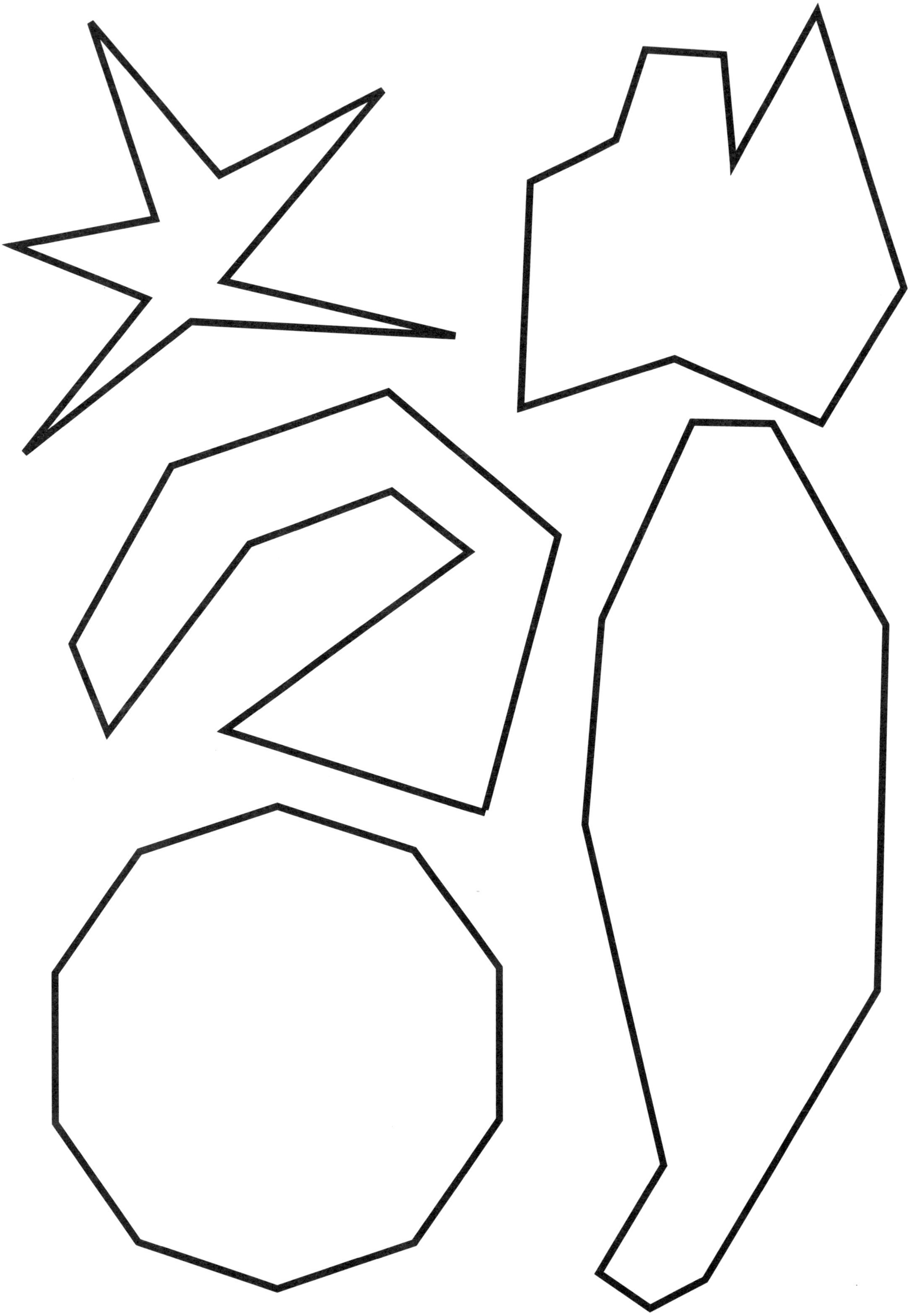

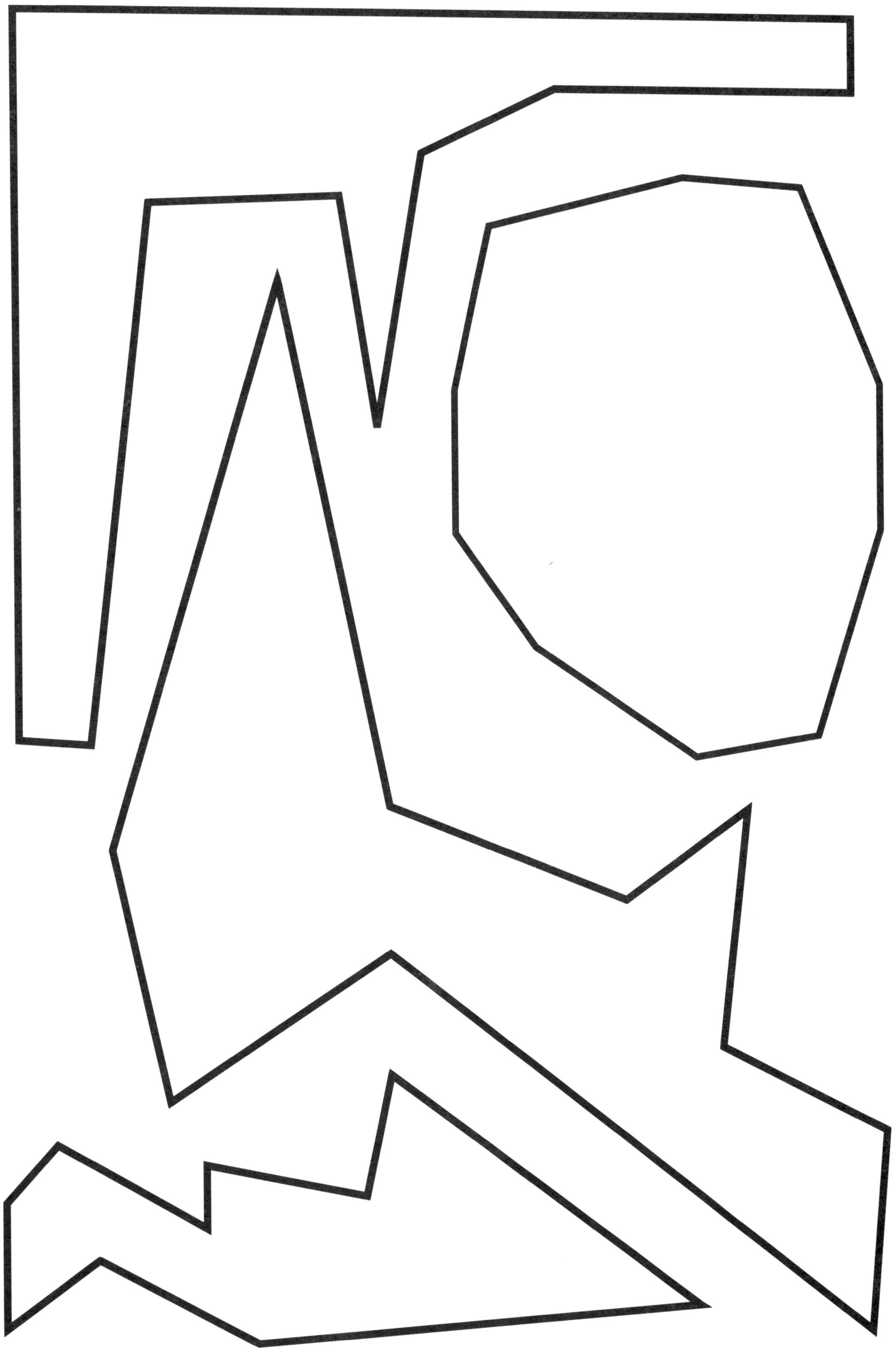

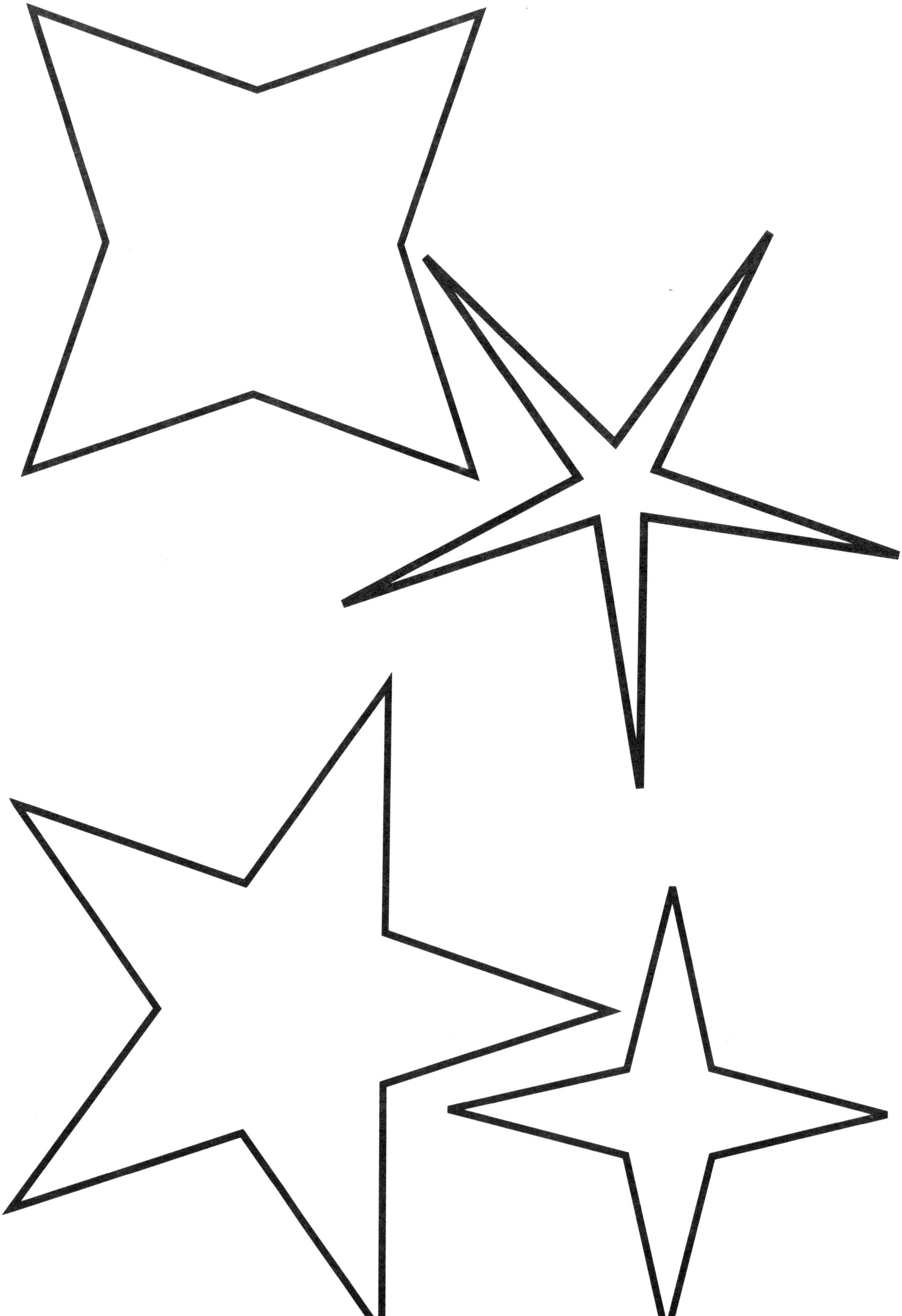

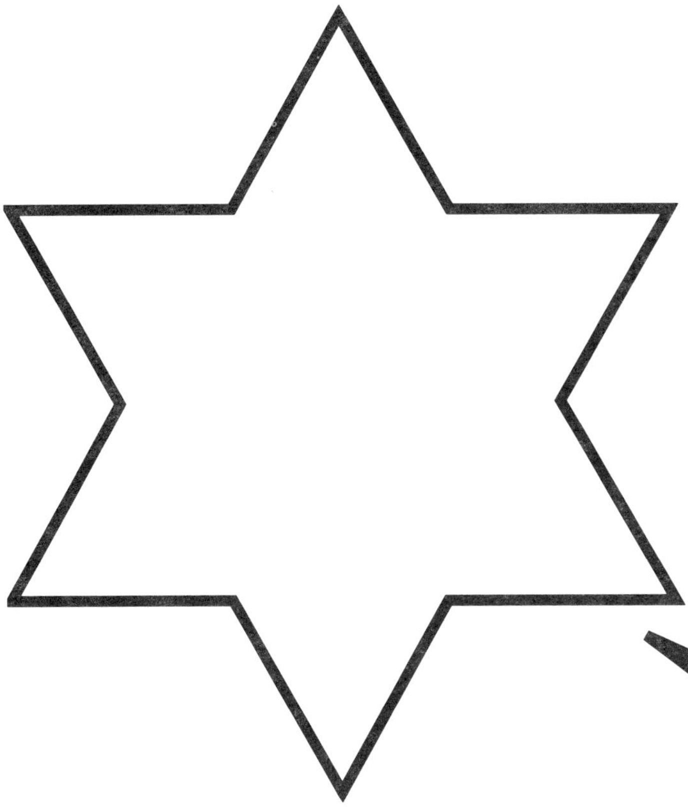
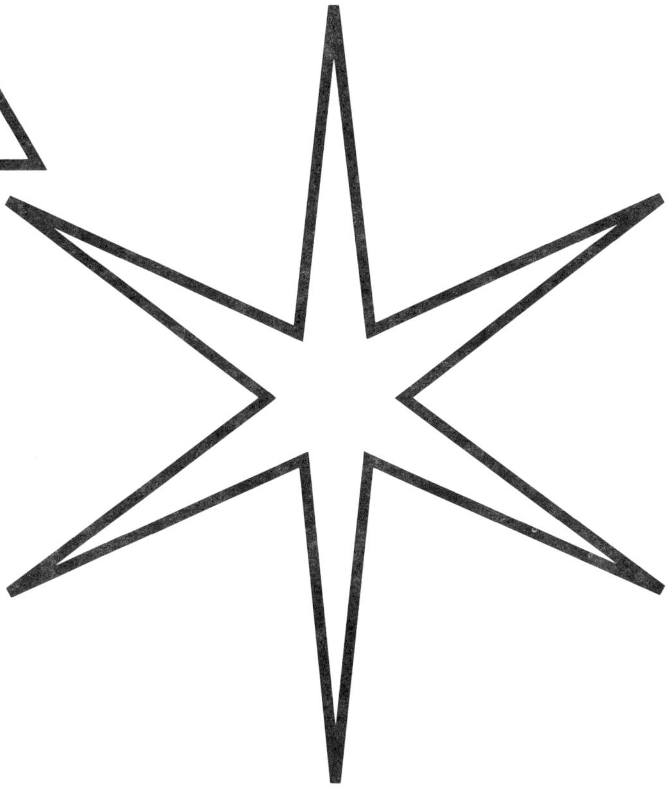
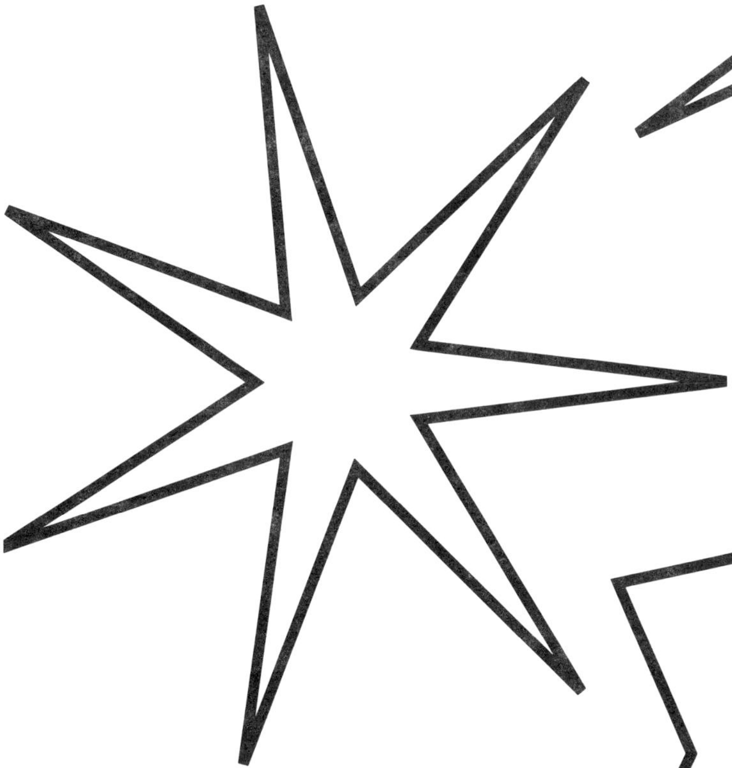
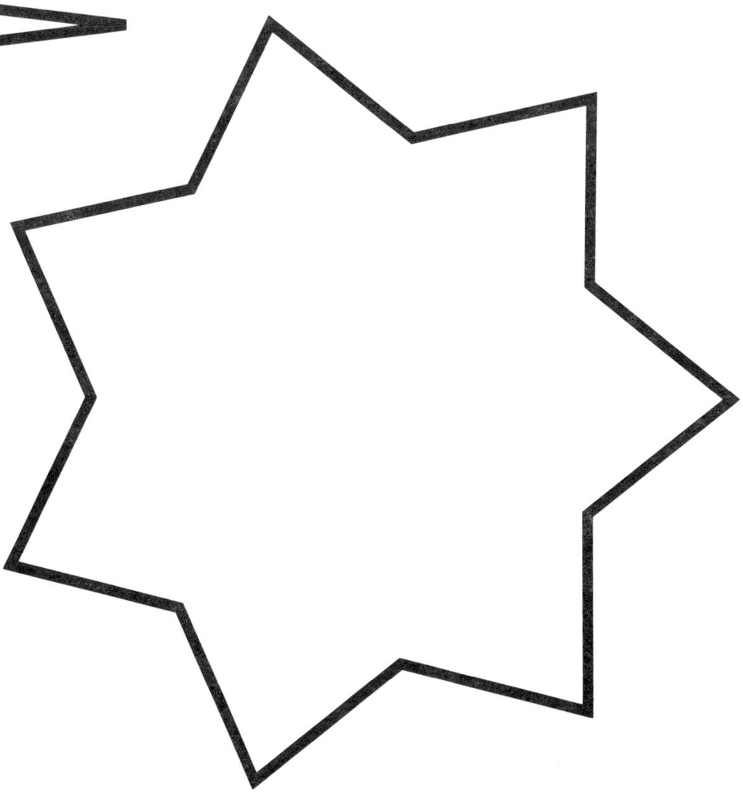

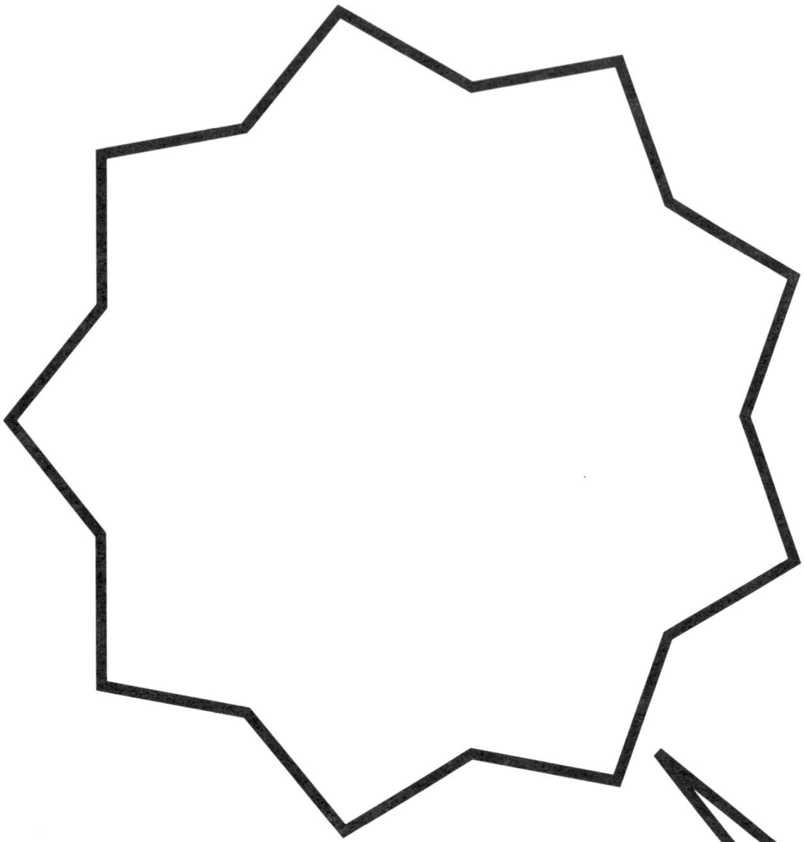

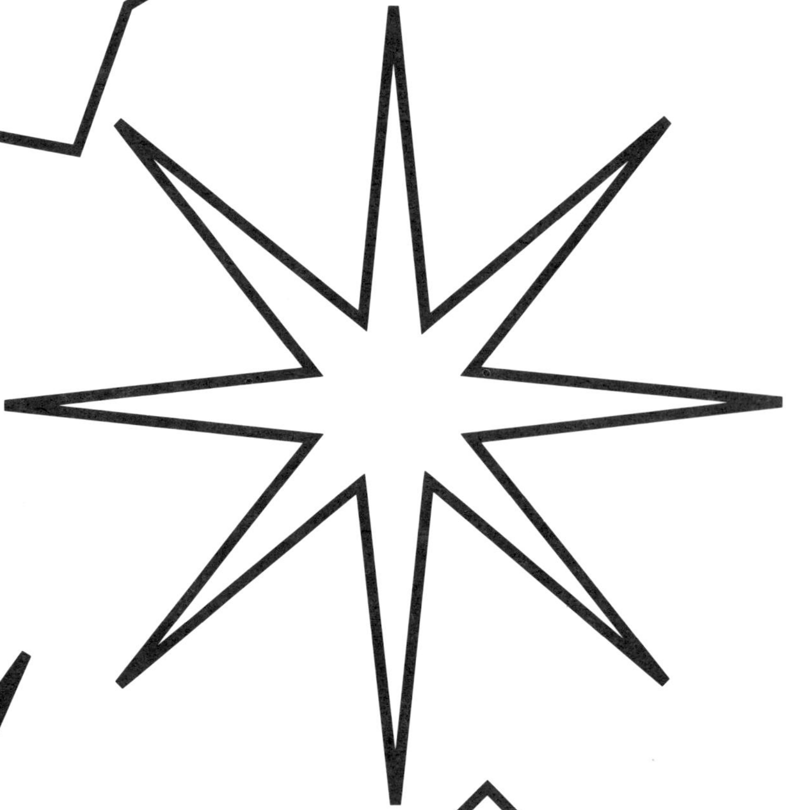

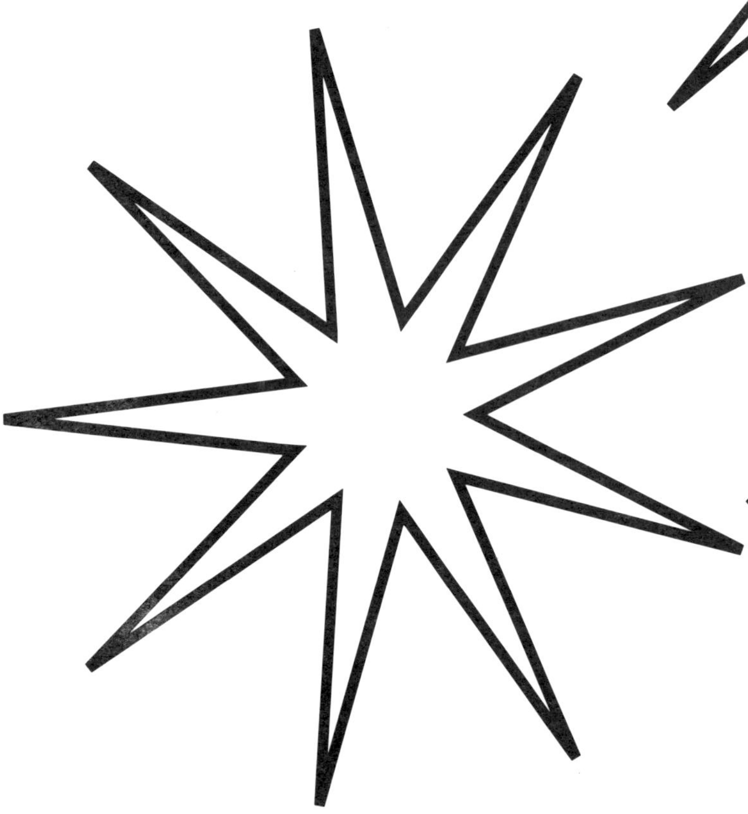

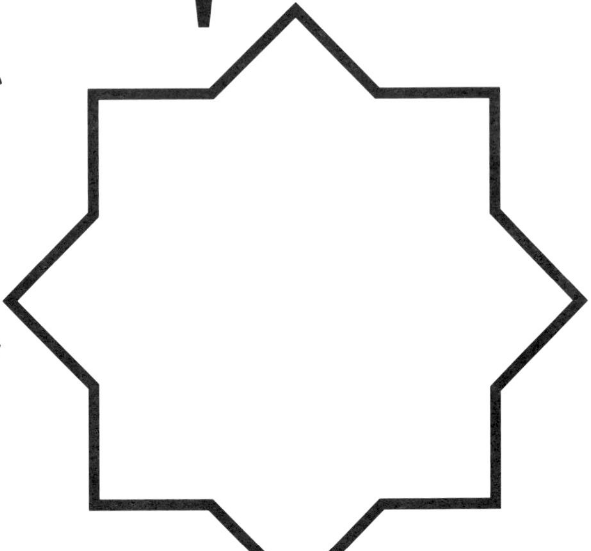

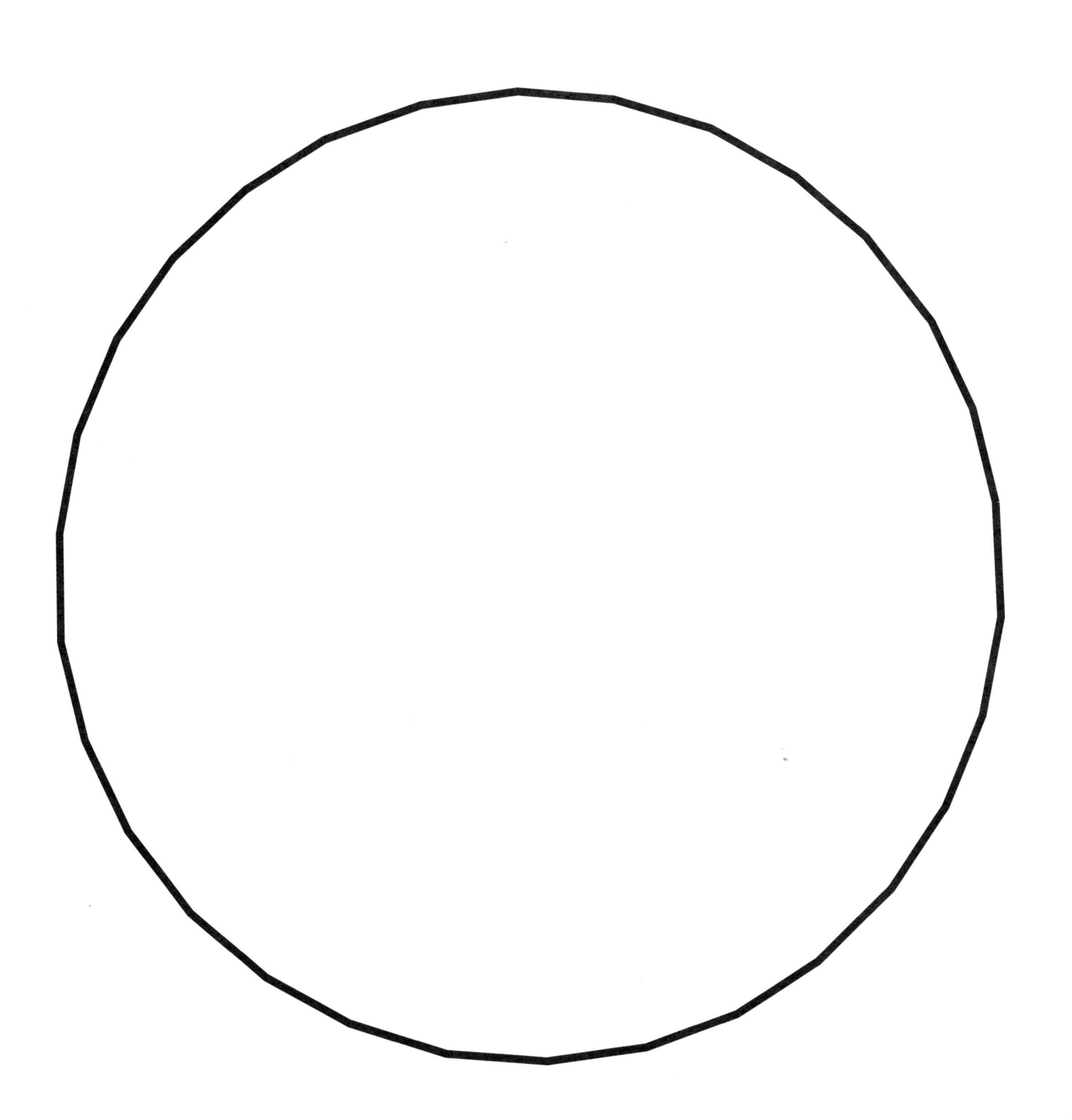

Books in this series

Rationale statement

The principles which govern this approach to mathematics teaching and learning are described in *Mapping mathematical meaning*. This theoretical statement provides the rationale for the way of teaching mathematics that is outlined in the other materials in this series.

Teaching and learning

Six topic books, **Base Ten**, *understanding the structure of the number system; Mathematics, a search for* **Patterns**; **Classification**, *a process for learning mathematics; Making sense of* **Fractions**; *The nature of* **Number**; *and* **Measuring Space**, give an account of these theories in action. These books are practical descriptions of activities and resources a teacher can use to establish a mathematical environment. They also discuss the types of response children make to such experiences, as well as map the development in children's mathematical thinking. Ongoing information about how to adapt and modify an activity to respond to children's developing thoughts provides the framework for continuity in learning. It also acts to challenge and support children's thinking beyond their existing parameters.

Managing the curriculum

A group of teachers implementing this approach have reflected on their classroom experiences. Their books provide practical information about how to manage aspects of the curriculum.

In these books, teachers share the structures and strategies they have developed to make the organisation and management of this approach to teaching effective and efficient.

Resourcing mathematics learning

In order to implement this way of teaching it is necessary to be well resourced. In particular, each child should have access to materials and activities which model the mathematics to be learnt. Many of these materials already exist in schools and are available from the various distributors of mathematics equipment. Sometimes teachers have needed to make their own resources to fit a specific task being set. To supplement the existing commercial supplies and, in the case of shape, to establish a more comprehensive set of examples, five books—**Triangles**; **Polygons**; **Fractions**; **Numbers and Numerals**; and **Dots and Grids**—provide pages which can be photocopied onto cardboard or paper, cut out and used to resource students' mathematics learning. They will save teachers the time and effort of making these resources for themselves.